C000075471

HEDGEHUGS

summersdale

An Hachette UK Company
www.hachette.co.uk

Summersdale Publishers Ltd
Part of Octopus Publishing Group Limited
Carmelite House
50 Victoria Embankment
LONDON
EC4Y 0DZ
UK

www.summersdale.com

Printed and bound in China

ISBN: 978-1-78783-258-9

Substantial discounts on bulk quantities of Summersdale books are available to corporations, professional associations and other organizations. For details contact general enquiries: telephone: +44 (0) 1243 771107 or email: enquiries@summersdale.com.

❤ INTRODUCTION ❤

Isn't it heart-warming when you see a little hedgehog roaming around outside? These gorgeous creatures, with their tiny button noses and cuter-than-cute ears, will brighten up the gloomiest days. Not only are they pretty little things, but they are fascinating to watch, too. Gentle and shy, yet resolutely determined, hedgehogs love to explore their surroundings and are fantastic foragers.

If you love hedgehogs, you'll love this book that showcases some of the most adorable hedgehogs ever. Enjoy!

WHEN YOU NEED
A LITTLE LOVE,
♥ GIVE A LITTLE ♥

HEDGEHUG

A HUG IS THE PERFECT GIFT —
ONE SIZE FITS ALL AND NOBODY
MINDS IF YOU EXCHANGE IT.

Ivern Ball

IF YOU'RE HOGGY AND
♥ YOU KNOW IT CLAP ♥

YOUR HANDS

HAPPINESS IS AN UNEXPECTED HUG.

Anonymous

♥ YOU'RE A ♥

TOP HOG

WHEN THE RIGHT PERSON HUGS YOU, IT'S LIKE MEDICINE. I'M SO GRATEFUL FOR THOSE FEW PEOPLE IN MY LIFE WHO ARE GOOD FOR MY SOUL.

Steve Maraboli

SO SQUISHY

♥ AND ♥

_____

SMOL

HUGGING: THE TRUEST FORM OF GIVING AND RECEIVING.

Carol CC Miller

♥ YOU'RE SO ♥

HOGGABLE

THEY INVENTED HUGS TO LET
PEOPLE KNOW YOU LOVE THEM
WITHOUT SAYING ANYTHING.

Bil Keane

♥ LIFE IS ♥

SWEET

AS THE NIGHTS GET COLDER, THE HUGS GET WARMER.

Anthony T. Hincks

♥ EVERY HOG HAS ♥

ITS DAY

A HUG MAKES YOU FEEL GOOD ALL DAY.

Kathleen Keating

HOG
♥ TIRED ♥

RECYCLE KISSES, HUGS AND SMILES;
THEY NEVER GO OUT OF STYLE
AND EVERYBODY NEEDS ONE.

Crystal DeLarm Clymer

HOT
♥ DIGGITY ♥
HOG

YOU CAN'T WRAP LOVE IN A BOX, BUT YOU CAN WRAP A PERSON IN A HUG.

Anonymous

♥ WHO LET THE ♥

HOGS OUT?

THE LOVE WE GIVE AWAY IS THE ONLY LOVE WE KEEP.

Elbert Hubbard

♥ IF I FITS, ♥

I SITS

LOVE IS A CIRCULAR EMOTION THAT SURROUNDS YOU, LIKE A HUG.

Jarod Kintz

VIH
(VERY IMPORTANT HOG)

LOVE IS THE OIL THAT EASES FRICTION, THE CEMENT THAT BINDS CLOSER TOGETHER, AND THE MUSIC THAT BRINGS HARMONY.

Eva Burrows

LIVING

♥ ON THE ♥

HEDGE

A HUG OVERCOMES ALL BOUNDARIES.
IT SPEAKS WORDS WITHIN THE
MIND THAT CANNOT BE SPOKEN.

Anonymous

A HOG IS

♥ A MAN'S ♥

BEST FRIEND

LAUGHING TOGETHER IS AS CLOSE AS YOU CAN GET TO A HUG WITHOUT TOUCHING.

Gina Barreca

THE DOG DAYS ARE OVER;

♥ THE HOG DAYS ARE ♥

HERE TO STAY

WE NEED FOUR HUGS A DAY FOR SURVIVAL. WE NEED EIGHT HUGS A DAY FOR MAINTENANCE. WE NEED TWELVE HUGS A DAY FOR GROWTH.

Virginia Satir

♥ LOOKING ♥

SHARP

NUPTIAL LOVE MAKETH MANKIND; FRIENDLY LOVE PERFECTETH IT.

Francis Bacon

♥ HAIR OF ♥

THE HOG

A HUG IS LIKE A BOOMERANG — YOU GET IT BACK RIGHT AWAY.

Bil Keane

IS IT A BAT?

IS IT A HOG?

♥ NO, IT'S ♥

BAT-HOG!

A HUG IS A HANDSHAKE FROM THE HEART.

Anonymous

ALL YOU NEED
IS LOVE... AND
A BABY HEDGEHOG
♥ ASLEEP IN ♥

YOUR HAND

LOVE... IT ENCOMPASSES EVERY BEING, SLOWLY EXPANDING TO EMBRACE ALL THAT EVER WILL BE.

Kahlil Gibran

AS SNUG

♥ AS A HOG ♥

IN A HUT

I HAVE LEARNED THAT THERE IS MORE POWER IN A GOOD STRONG HUG THAN IN A THOUSAND MEANINGFUL WORDS.

Ann Hood

♥ LET SLEEPING ♥

HOGS LIE

HUGS CAN DO GREAT AMOUNTS OF GOOD.

Diana, Princess of Wales

#HEDGEHOGLIFE

PEOPLE... WHO LOVE YOU... PUT
THEIR ARMS AROUND YOU AND LOVE
YOU WHEN YOU'RE NOT SO LOVABLE.

Deb Caletti

♥ I LOVE YOU ♥

THHIISSS MUCH!

A HUG SHOWS COMPASSION. A HUG
BRINGS DELIGHT. A HUG CHARMS THE
SENSES. A HUG TOUCHES THE SOUL.

Anonymous

If you're interested in finding out more about our books, find us on Facebook at **Summersdale Publishers** and follow us on Twitter at **@Summersdale**.

www.summersdale.com

IMAGE CREDITS